The Urbana Free Library

To renew: call **217-367-4057**
or go to **urbanafreelibrary.org**
and select **My Account**

A Look at
SAND, SILT, AND MUD

Cecelia H. Brannon

 Enslow Publishing
101 W. 23rd Street
Suite 240
New York, NY 10011
USA
enslow.com

Published in 2016 by Enslow Publishing, LLC
101 W. 23rd Street, Suite 240, New York, NY 10011

Library of Congress Cataloging-in-Publication Data

Brannon, Cecelia H., author
 A look at sand, silt, and mud / Cecelia H. Brannon
    pages cm. — (The rock cycle)
 Audience: Ages 8+
 Audience: Grades 4 to 6.
 ISBN 978-0-7660-7334-0 (library binding)
 ISBN 978-0-7660-7332-6 (pbk.)
 ISBN 978-0-7660-7333-3 (6-pack)
 1. Sediments (Geology)—Juvenile literature. 2. Sand—Juvenile literature. 3. Geochemical cycles—Juvenile literature. I.
Title.
 QE471.2.B67 2016
 553.6—dc23
                        2015029181
Printed in the United States of America

To Our Readers: We have done our best to make sure all websites in this book were active and appropriate when we went to press. However, the author and the publisher have no control over and assume no liability for the material available on those websites or any websites they may link to. Any comments or suggestions can be sent by e-mail to customerservice@enslow.com.

Photo Credits: Throughout book, cover, p. 1 Piotr Grymkowski/Shutterstock.com (sand background), Creative Nature Media/Shutterstock.com (silt layers), Nito/Shutterstock.com (sand), Dvorko Sergey/Shutterstock.com (mud), NelliGal/Shutterstock.com (silt), Christine Yarusi (series logo, four-rock dingbat); p. 4 Marina Khlybova/Shutterstock.com; p. 6 Maxim Tupikov/Shutterstock.com (top), Diana Taliun/Shutterstock.com (bottom); p. 7 Dr. Morley Read/Shutterstock.com (top), Dvorko Sergey/Shutterstock.com (bottom); p. 8 Lukiyanova Natalia/frenta/Shutterstock.com; p. 9 ZeWrestler/Wikimedia Commons/Rockcycle2.jpg/public domain; p. 10 Education Images/Geography Photos/UIG via Getty Images; p. 11 © iStockphoto.com/lelpado; p. 12 Jeremy Horner/LightRocket via Getty Images; p. 13 MC_PP/Shutterstock.com; p. 14 MOHAMMED ABED/AFP/Getty Images; p. 15 Zygotehaasnobrain/Shutterstock.com; p. 16 Joseph Sohm/Shutterstock.com; p. 17 Mayall/Ullstein bid via Getty Images; p. 18 Claudiovidri/Shutterstock.com; p. 19 BarryTuck/Shutterstock.com (top), Yongyuan Dai/Moment/Getty Images (bottom); p. 21 Bruce Rolff/Shutterstock.com (top), Mike Brake/Shutterstock.com (bottom); p. 22 Susan R. Serna/Shutterstock.com (top) gnomeandi/Shutterstock.com (middle), Tata Chen/Shutterstock.com (bottom); p. 24 Vadim Petrakov/Shutterstock.com (top), FloridaStock/Shutterstock.com (bottom); p. 25 Alison Hancock/Shutterstock.com (top), Sestovic/Shutterstock.com (bottom); p. 26 Roman Sigaev/Shutterstock.com (top), Halfpoint/Shutterstock.com (bottom); p. 27 Len44ik/Shutterstock.com; p. 28 Ben Carlon/Shutterstock.com (top), Anton_Ivanov/Shutterstock.com (bottom); p. 29 claires/Shutterstock.com (top), Steve Lagreca/Shutterstock.com (bottom).

Contents

Sand dunes stretch as far as the eye can see under the blue sky in a desert in Kazakhstan.

What Are
SAND, SILT, AND MUD?

Soil and rock cover the surface of the planet Earth. Over time, that soil and rock break down to form clasts. Clasts are small broken pieces of rock. Sand, silt, and mud are the clasts that form from metamorphic, sedimentary, and igneous rocks.

Grain Size

Clasts are named for the size of the grains from which they formed. Sand is made from large coarse grains. It is formed from small bits of rock and is most commonly found on beaches. A grain of sand is usually 0.002 to 0.08 inches (0.05 to 2 millimeters) in diameter.

Sand may feel soft beneath your feet at the beach, but it's actually the roughest of the clasts.

Did You Know?

A beach pail can hold more than three billion grains of sand!

Silt is also made from bits of rock. Most commonly found along streams and riverbeds, it is much finer than sand. A grain of silt can be 0.00008 to 0.002 inches (0.002 to 0.05 millimeters) in diameter.

Mud is a mixture of water and soil. It is the finest clast and can be found anywhere.

A canoe sits on silt along the Cononaco River in Ecuador.

Mud is a watery clast.

The Rock Cycle

The rock cycle is the process by which old rocks break down to form new rocks. Sand, silt, and mud and the rock cycle go hand in hand. They could not exist without each other.

Earth is constructed of several layers. The crust, where we live, is 97 percent rock. Below that is the mantle, which consists of liquid magma. And beneath the mantle are the outer core, made of melted metal, and the inner core, made of solid metal.

The rock cycle begins when magma from the mantle rises to the surface. There, it cools and hardens, which forms igneous rocks. Through weathering, igneous rocks wear down over

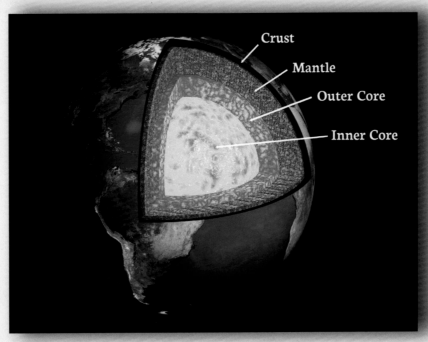

Crust

Mantle

Outer Core

Inner Core

The rock cycle operates through Earth's layers.

time and become sand, silt, and mud. These materials mix with other matter like dirt to become sediment, which settles into layers over time. Pressure is applied to these layers and forces out any water to create sedimentary rocks. When heat and pressure changes the minerals in sedimentary or igneous rocks, they become metamorphic rocks. Through earthquakes and other natural events, rocks are forced underground, where they melt into magma. And the rock cycle begins again!

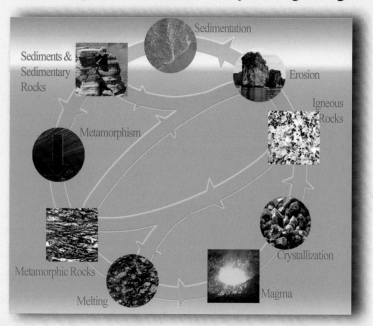

This diagram illustrates the rock cycle, which turns sand, silt, and mud into sediment and, later, sedimentary rock.

How Are
SAND, SILT, AND MUD
Formed?

Rocks are strong, but wind and water can be stronger. Erosion is one of the ways in which rocks break down to become sand, silt, and mud. After the rocks are broken down, forces like wind and running water carry them away.

Weathering is another process that breaks down rocks. Rocks expand when they get hot

These rocks in Andalusia, Spain, have been eroded and weathered over time by wind and water.

and contract when they cool. This stretching and shrinking weathers the rock. This is physical, or mechanical, weathering. Physical weathering also occurs when forces like wind, water, and ice weaken the surface of a rock and break it down.

Another kind of weathering, chemical weathering, happens when elements, such as oxygen, interact with a rock's minerals and change them.

When plants grow in cracks in rocks, they help further break down the rocks into sand, silt, or mud.

This mountain range in India shows signs of weathering.

Becoming Sand, Silt, or Mud

Rocks go through a long journey to become sand, silt, or mud. Rain or flowing water washes the broken rock pieces into streams and rivers, which carry them into oceans and seas. As the pieces travel, they bump into each other and are rubbed by water. This makes them smaller and smoother over time.

Different amounts and types of erosion determine which clast the rock pieces will become. Lots of erosion creates mud's fine grains, while less erosion creates the rough texture of sand.

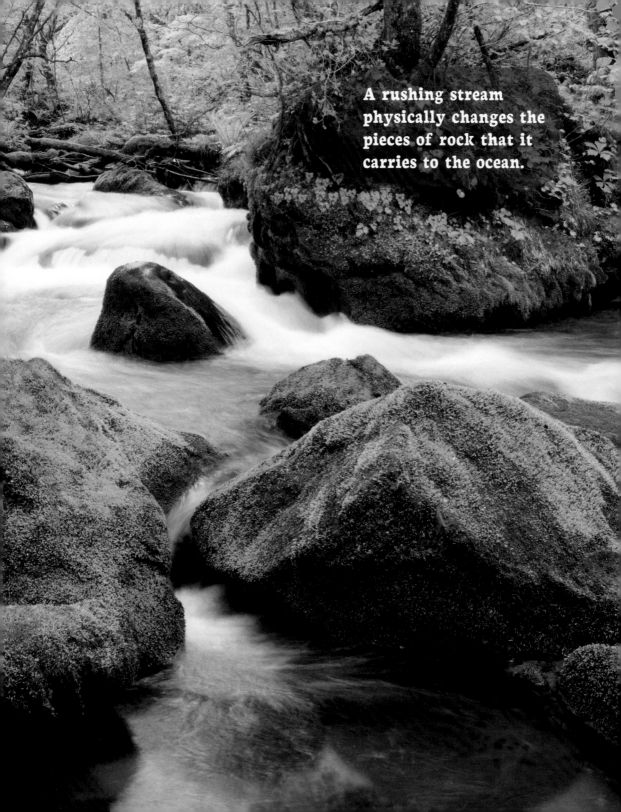

A rushing stream physically changes the pieces of rock that it carries to the ocean.

Did You Know?

Seashells are often brought in by the tide during a storm. Over time, the sea will break down the shells to form sand.

Once the pieces of rock have become clasts, the wind can carry them. Before, they were too heavy to be carried by anything other than water. Once they are lighter and smaller, strong winds can carry clasts for miles (kilometers) and rub them the same way water does. This causes the grains to differ in size and shape. The clasts usually make it to the ocean.

This is what sand looks like under a microscope. You can see the tiny pieces of shell and rock.

Did You Know?

Glaciers also cause erosion. Sand and silt can get caught in the ice. As the glacier melts, it deposits the sediment. Glaciers can even carry entire rocks across continents!

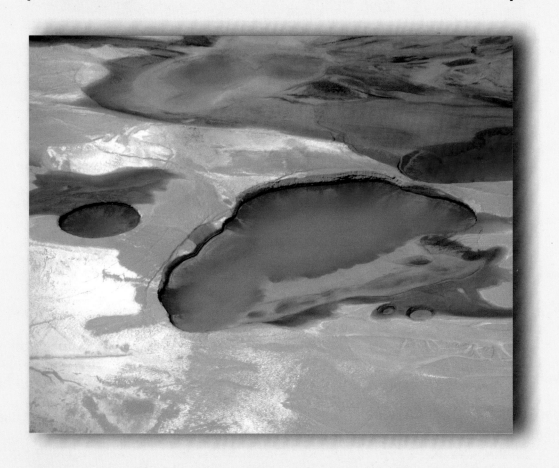

Did You Know?

This dust storm in the Australian outback is one way that clasts travel. Dust is what we call silt when it is in the air.

Transforming Into Sedimentary Rock

When sand, silt, and mud reach the ocean, they sink to the bottom. The bigger grains fall first, and the lighter ones lay on top of them to form layers. These grains mix with other materials, such as shells.

Did You Know?

Beaches are not the only places you can find sand. Deserts form when wind blows sand into dry areas.

Over time, the layers of grains and other sediments become hard and form sedimentary rocks. Different sediments create different kinds of rock. Sand creates sandstone, silt forms silt-stone, and mud creates a stone called shale. These stones have been used in building for centuries.

Sandstone is a sedimentary rock that is created when sand is pressed together under pressure. It is often used in building.

Angkor-Wat in Cambodia was built in the tenth century. Made of sandstone, it is still standing today.

Characteristics of
SAND, SILT, AND MUD

The amount of erosion that has occurred determines the texture and size of sand grains. A sand grain that is smooth has probably traveled far, whereas a grain that is rough probably has not.

Silt mostly forms through the weathering of rock pieces. Silt grains are finer than sand. Silt is so light and small that water and wind can move it around easily. Silt grains are always smooth, unlike sand grains, which can be rough. Silt is often found in rivers and along the banks of streams or the shallow part of the ocean.

Mud is formed when weathered, broken pieces of rock and the remains of dead plants and animals mix with water. It is most commonly found around bodies of water. When animals drink from a watering hole or a lake, they walk on the soil around the water's edge, which breaks the soil into even smaller pieces.

Did You Know?

The color of sand depends on what it is made from. White or tan sand is made from broken down shells or coral. Red sand is made from pieces of garnet. Black sand comes from black rocks like obsidian.

Did You Know?

Silt is so fine is it often called rock flour.

Mud often has pieces of plant material, as well as sand or silt, in it. This means mud is rich in nutrients, which makes it fertile. Mud is good for growing vegetables and other plants.

Did You Know?

Animals love the mud. In hot places like India and Africa, it helps to keep them cool.

Rice sprouts grow in a muddy paddy.

Why Are
SAND, SILT, AND MUD
Important?

Sand, silt, and mud are important parts of the environment. They change Earth's surface by creating various landforms. People have also found many uses for these different kinds of clasts.

Effects on the Environment

Rivers carry large amounts of sand, silt, and mud. When a river flows into the ocean, it leaves sediment behind. This sediment can create a big fan-shaped area called a delta.

Silt and mud can be found in places called tidal flats. These are areas that are covered by the ocean's tide twice a day. These tides leave a lot of silt behind. These areas create a rich environment for animals such as clams, worms, turtles, snakes, otters, and shorebirds. Mud is also found in swamps.

The Okavango Delta is in Botswana, Africa. It is considered one of the Seven Natural Wonders of Africa.

Sand, Silt, and Mud Are Useful

Sand has an important role in the rock cycle, but it is also important to people. Sand is used to create sandbags to keep back floodwater. Cement and bricks are made from sand.

These grizzly bears are walking on a tidal flat in Alaska.

Why Are **SAND, SILT, AND MUD** Important?

Workers pour cement to fix a sidewalk. Another worker lays bricks to build a home. Both of these materials are made from sand.

Glass is made from sand that has been heated at high temperatures. Roofing shingles also often have sand in them.

Sandpaper is used to smooth surfaces such as wood and plaster. Its rough surface gently wears away rough areas just like weathering and erosion have worn down rocks to create sand.

Many skyscrapers use glass in their construction.

Sandy soil is even good for growing plants, such as watermelon, peanuts, corn, and spinach.

Silt and mud are great for growing things. Silt is often added to soil to make it more suitable for crops. All the nutrients from decaying plants and animals make mud fertile.

This person is removing paint from an old chair using sandpaper.

Did You Know?

Sandcastles are a common sight on the beach. Many beaches around the world even host sandcastle-building competitions. According to the Guinness Book of World Records, the tallest sandcastle built to date was in Rio de Janeiro, Brazil. It was 41 feet and 3.67 inches (12.59 m) tall!

Did You Know?

The unique red color of baseball fields is created when silt is added to the soil.

Mud is also used in construction. Mud bricks have been used for thousands of years all over the world.

This mud brick village in the Dakhla Oasis in Egypt was built in the middle ages.

Why Are **SAND, SILT, AND MUD** Important?

Surprisingly, some people actually use mud to get clean. They put on mud masks to deeply cleanse their faces or even take baths in thermal mud springs!

The nutrients found in mud are good for the skin.

Sand, silt, and mud may not seem exciting, but they are an important part of the rock cycle. Without sand, silt, and mud, we would not have sedimentary rocks, not to mention bricks or glass. Sand, silt, and mud even help plants to grow! Without them, the rock cycle would not be able to carry on. Sand, silt, and mud are an important part of our life on Earth!

The Painted Desert in Arizona is a popular tourist attraction. Here, you can see the rock cycle at work: sand, silt, and sedimentary rocks are all common sights.

Glossary

clasts–Small broken pieces of rock.

delta–A fan-shaped pile of sediment that collects at the mouth of a river.

erosion–The wearing away of land over time. Erosion is also the part of the rock cycle in which bits of matter become sediment.

fertile–Good for making and growing things.

igneous rocks–Hot liquid underground minerals that have cooled and hardened.

metamorphic–Having to do with rock that has been changed by heat and heavy weight.

minerals–Natural elements that are not animals, plants, or other living things.

sediment–Sand, silt, or mud carried by wind or water.

sedimentary–Having to do with layers of stones, sand, or mud that have been pressed together to form rock.

tidal flats– Land that is covered by the tide twice per day.

weathering– The breaking up of rock by water, wind, and chemical forces.

Further Reading

BOOKS

Bair, Diane, and Emily Sohn. *Pebbles, Sand, and Silt: The Neighbor's Garden.* Chicago: Norwood House Paper Editions, 2012.

Lawrence, Ellen. *Is Sand a Rock?* New York: Bearport Publishing. 2014.

Lindeen, Mary. *Investigating the Rock Cycle.* New York: Lerner Publications, 2015.

Pendergast, George. *The Rock Cycle at Work.* New York: Gareth-Stevens Publishing, 2015.

WEBSITES

ScienceViews.com
scienceviews.com/geology/rocks.html
Read more about the rock cycle.

History for Kids: Soil Types
historyforkids.org/learn/environment/soiltypes.html
Learn about different soil types.

Discovery Education: The Dirt on Soil
school.discoveryeducation.com/schooladventures/soil/name_soil.html
Discover the different wildlife that lives in soil and go on an interactive adventure that teaches about soil.

Index